To Dr. Jan Knippers Black
Best regards,
Oscar Arias S.
2002

HORIZONS OF PEACE

THE COSTA RICAN CONTRIBUTION TO THE PEACE PROCESS IN CENTRAL AMERICA

OSCAR ARIAS SANCHEZ

CONTENTS

Oil painting of President Oscar Arias by Antonio Sereix.

Oscar Arias unites actions with words. His ideals are the product of extraordinary capability, visionary spirit, vast experience, and a profound sense of compassion. These attributes were particularly visible during the 1986 electoral campaign for the Presidency of the Republic.

Children participating in the campaign for the Presidency of the Republic.

With his wife, Margarita, and his children, Oscar Felipe and Sylvia Eugenia.

With José Figueres.

With his wife, Margarita Penón.

With José Figueres.

A hug from Margarita during the confirmation of his candidacy for the Presidency of the Republic.

When electoral victory was certain.

With Margarita and the former Presidents of Costa Rica: José Joaquín Trejos, Rodrigo Carazo, José Figueres, Mario Echandi, and Daniel Oduber. All supported Arias' proposals for peace.

During Arias' inauguration at the National Stadium. Present are members of the four branches of Costa Rican government as well as President Luis Alberto Monge and First Lady Doris Yankelewitz de Monge.

During the inauguration gala in the National Theatre, San José. Accompanying President Arias are Presidents José Napoleón Duarte of El Salvador, Belisario Betancur of Colombia, Julio María Sanguinetti of Uruguay, José Azcona of Honduras, León Febres of Ecuador, Raúl Alfonsín of Argentina, Erick Arturo del Valle of Panamá, and Marco Vinicio Cerezo of Guatemala.

PROLOGUE

HORIZONS OF PEACE PROVIDES A WRITTEN AND PICTORIAL ACCOUNT OF THE GENESIS AND DEVELOPMENT OF THE ARIAS PEACE PLAN. THROUGH VIVID PHOTOGRAPHY AND EXCERPTS OF SPEECHES MADE BY PRESIDENT ARIAS, THE BOOK HIGHLIGHTS THE EVENTS THAT LED TO THE SIGNING OF THE PEACE PLAN ON 7 AUGUST, 1987. HORIZONS OF PEACE, HOWEVER, DOES MORE THAN JUST RETRACE THE STEPS OF HISTORY. IN ITS DEPICTION OF THE CENTRAL AMERICAN PEACE PROCESS, IT ALSO SPEAKS OF THE ADVANCEMENT OF PEACE THROUGHOUT THE WORLD AND MAKES AN APPEAL FOR INTERNATIONAL COOPERATION TO SUSTAIN POLITICAL AND ECONOMIC STABILITY IN THE THIRD WORLD.

THE ESTABLISHMENT OF LASTING PEACE IN THE CENTRAL AMERICAN REGION IS A CONTINUOUS STRUGGLE. THE END OF THE NICARAGUAN CIVIL WAR AND THE MORE RECENT CESSATION OF THE ARMED CONFLICT IN EL SALVADOR INDICATE GROWING STABILITY IN THE REGION. HOWEVER, THERE IS GREAT NEED FOR RENEWED COMMITMENT TO THE PEACE ACCORDS TO ENSURE FURTHER PROGRESS. INTERNATIONAL SUPPORT IS CRUCIAL TO OVERCOME THE MANY YEARS OF KILLING, INJUSTICE AND DESPAIR WE HAVE SUFFERED.

THE STRUGGLE FOR LASTING PEACE DOES NOT APPLY ONLY TO CENTRAL AMERICA. VIOLENCE CAN BE FUND AROUND THE WORLD IN A MYRIAD OF FORMS: WAR, MILITARISM, DISCRIMINATION, DISEASE, ILLITERACY, ENVIRONMENTAL DESTRUCTION.... ACHIEVING THE ERADICATION OF THESE EVILS IS THE RESPONSIBILITY OF ALL HUMANKIND.

THE ARIAS FOUNDATION FOR PEACE AND HUMAN PROGRESS JOINS IN THE INTERNATIONAL STRUGGLE AGAINST VIOLENCE BY SPONSORING THIS FIRST ENGLISH EDITION OF HORIZONS OF PEACE. WE BELIEVE THAT THIS BOOK IS A TESTIMONY OF HOW PEACE AND DEMOCRACY ARE BOTH NECESSARY AND POSSIBLE ON A GLOBAL SCALE.

THE ARIAS FOUNDATION ATTEMPTS TO ERADICATE VIOLENCE IN OTHER WAYS AS WELL. ESTABLISHED BY OSCAR ARIAS WITH THE MONETARY AWARD RECEIVED FROM THE 1987 NOBEL PEACE PRIZE, THE FOUNDATION IS DEDICATED TO ADVANCING THE IDEALS THAT INSPIRED THE ARCHITECTS OF THE CENTRAL AMERICAN PEACE PLAN. RECOGNIZED AS THE FIRST COMMUNITY FOUNDATION IN CENTRAL AMERICA, THIS NON-PROFIT INSTITUTION SERVES THE MOST NEEDY SECTORS OF OUR SOCIETIES.

THE FOUNDATION RECEIVES FINANCIAL SUPPORT FROM DIVERSE SOURCES —SUCH AS GOVERNMENTS, NON-GOVERNMENTAL INSTITUTIONS, INDIVIDUALS, AND OTHER PUBLIC AND PRIVATE ENTITIES— TO CONTINUE ITS PURSUIT OF PEACE, FREEDOM, DEMOCRACY, RESPECT FOR HUMAN RIGHTS, THE STRENGTHENING OF CIVIL SOCIETY, AND EQUALITY OF OPPORTUNITY IN THE REGION.

TO ACCOMPLISH ITS MISSION, *THE FOUNDATION* HAS ESTABLISHED THREE PROGRAMS. *THE CENTRE FOR HUMAN PROGRESS* ADVANCES THE PRINCIPLE THAT DEVELOPMENT CAN ONLY BE ACHIEVED WHERE PEACE, LIBERTY, AND EQUALITY COEXIST IN A HEALTHY AND SECURE ENVIRONMENT. IT STRIVES TO IMPROVE WOMEN'S ACCESS TO LAND, TO ENCOURAGE RESPECT FOR WOMEN'S RIGHTS, AND TO FURTHER REGIONAL OPPORTUNITIES FOR SUSTAINABLE ECONOMIC DEVELOPMENT.

THE CENTRE FOR PEACE AND RECONCILIATION ADVOCATES DEMILITARIZATION AND DISARMAMENT, AS WELL AS THE PREVENTION AND PEACEFUL RESOLUTION OF CONFLICTS. IT ESPOUSES A CONCEPT OF SECURITY WHICH IS MORE ENCOMPASSING THAN TRADITIONAL NOTIONS WHICH ADVOCATE MILITARY BALANCE AND PREPAREDNESS. INSTEAD, IT LINKS HUMAN WELFARE TO THE ABSENCE OF FEAR, VIOLENCE, MILITARISM, POVERTY, DISEASE, AND OPPRESSION.

THE CENTRE FOR PHILANTHROPY PROMOTES THE APPLICATION OF MODERN CONCEPTS OF PHILANTHROPY BY NON-GOVERNMENTAL AND NON-PROFIT ORGANIZATIONS IN THE REGION. IT IS DEDICATED TO THE ESTABLISHMENT OF MORE EFFICIENT MECHANISMS WHICH DIRECT RESOURCES FROM THE PRIVATE AND PUBLIC SECTORS TOWARDS DEVELOPMENT.

WE HOPE THAT HORIZONS OF PEACE DEEPENS YOUR UNDERSTANDING AND INSPIRES YOU TO JOIN US AT ARIAS FOUNDATION IN THE STRUGGLE FOR GLOBAL PEACE.

MARIA EUGENIA DE COTTER
DIRECTOR
ARIAS FOUNDATION FOR PEACE AND HUMAN PROGRESS

SAN JOSÉ, COSTA RICA, JUNE 1994

INTRODUCTION

TODAY CENTRAL AMERICA IS UNDERGOING A SEVERE POLITICAL, ECONOMIC AND SOCIAL CRISIS. HOWEVER ITS PROBLEMS ARE NOT NEW. THEY ARE THE PRODUCT OF UNJUST STRUCTURES, DATING FROM COLONIAL TIMES, WHICH CONTRIBUTE TO THE RECURRENCE OF MILITARY REGIMES, THE PERSISTENCE OF INEQUALITY, ILLITERACY, AND DISEASE, AND THE PERPETUATION OF POVERTY AND DESPERATION.

IN RECENT YEARS, CENTRAL AMERICAN HARDSHIPS HAVE REACHED INTOLERABLE PROPORTIONS. DESPITE THE IDEOLOGICAL RETRENCHMENT OF THE LATE EIGHTIES, FEAR AND CONFLICT CONTINUE TO DISRUPT THESE SOCIETIES. LATELY, THE SITUATION HAS RELAPSED INTO GUERRILLA WARFARE IN AT LEAST ONE OF THE FIVE NATIONS OF THE ISTHMUS. ONCE AGAIN, THE REGION'S DEVELOPMENT IS POSTPONED, IF NOT REVERSED, BY VIOLENCE AND DISCORD. WHILE WAR CONTINUE, IT IMPOSSIBLE FOR OUR PEOPLES TO WORK TOGETHER IN SEARCH OF THE PEACE AND PROSPERITY THEY DESERVE.

SUCH INSIGHT SHAPED THE PROPOSAL THAT, UNDER THE TITLE, «A TIME

FOR PEACE», WAS PRESENTED IN SAN JOSÉ ON 15 FEBRUARY 1987, TO THE

PRESIDENTS OF EL SALVADOR, GUATEMALA AND HONDURAS, BY THE

COSTA RICAN HEAD OF STATE DR. OSCAR ARIAS SANCHEZ. THIS WAS HIS

FIRST ATTEMPT TO INITIATE A «PROCESS TO ESTABLISH A FIRM AND LAST-

ING PEACE IN CENTRAL AMERICA». THIS PROPOSAL REFLECTED THE POPU-

LAR WILL AS EXPRESSED BY THE COSTA RICAN PRESIDENT WHEN HE TOOK

OFFICE ON 8 MAY 1986. ON THAT OCCASION HE

DECLARED:

«WE WILL FAITHFULLY FULFIL OUR COMMITMENT TO

DEFEND AND STRENGTHEN PEACE AND NEUTRALITY. WE

WILL MAINTAIN COSTA RICA'S NEUTRALITY AND WE WILL

STRUGGLE, WITH DIPLOMATIC AND POLITICAL MEANS, TO

ACHIEVE AN END TO THE FIGHTING BETWEEN BROTHERS

IN CENTRAL AMERICA».

ULTIMATELY, THE PROPOSAL BECAME THE CENTRAL AMERICAN PEACE

PLAN, KNOWN AS ESQUIPULAS II. IT WAS APPROVED IN GUATEMALA ON 7

AUGUST 1987, BY ALL OF THE CENTRAL AMERICAN PRESIDENTS, INCLUD-

ING DANIEL ORTEGA OF NICARAGUA. THE PEACE PLAN IS THE CULMINA-

TION OF A LONG PROCESS OF NEGOTIATIONS IN WHOSE ORIGINS MANY LATIN AMERICAN NATIONS TOOK PART, NOTABLY COLOMBIA, MEXICO, PANAMA AND VENEZUELA, WHICH FORMED THE CONTADORA GROUP. BUT THE PLAN IS PRIMARILY THE PRODUCT OF THE PERSEVERANCE OF ONE MAN WHO UPHOLDS PEACE AS ONE OF MANKIND'S SUPREME VALUES: DR. OSCAR ARIAS SANCHEZ.

THIS BOOK PRESENTS THE READER WITH AN INSIGHT OF THE INCEP-TION AND DEVELOPMENT OF THE COSTA RICAN PRESIDENT'S INITIATIVE, COMBINING TEXTS FROM PRESIDENT ARIAS' SPEECHES WITH PHOTOGRAPHS DEPICT-ING HIS CAREER AND STRUGGLE FOR PEACE.

HORIZONS OF PEACE SENDS, TO CENTRAL AMERICA AND TO THE WORLD, A MESSAGE OF CONFIDENCE REGARDING THE ADVENT OF PEACE. IT CAN BE A REALITY, BOTH HERE AND ELSE-WHERE IN THE WORLD.

JORGE EMILIO REGIDOR MATTEY

SAN JOSÉ, 16 NOVEMBER 1989.

DEN NORSKE NOBELKOMITÉ

HAR OVERENSSTEMMENDE MED REGLENE I DET AV

ALFRED NOBEL

DEN 27. NOVEMBER 1895 OPPRETTEDE TESTAMENTE TILDELT

OSCAR ARIAS SÁNCHEZ

NOBELS FREDSPRIS FOR 1987

OSLO, 10. DESEMBER 1987

BACKGROUND

ORIGINS OF THE CONFLICT

A LAND OF CONTRASTS

Central America: how ironic that such a small geographic region bore a crisis so severe that it surpassed regional boundaries.

The Central American isthmus is an area of great contrasts. Disparities exist among the five countries and among the people that inhabit them: there are nations in Central America where human rights are defended, others where they are violated on an everyday basis; there are nations where fratricidal struggles pervade both towns and cities, others where peaceful coexistence is the norm. Among its peoples are musicians and poets of superior intellectual capacity beside thousands upon thousands of illiterate men and women; there are painters and sculptors whose artistic expressions have transcended borders, just as there are dictators who have sorpassed boundaries with expressions of cruelty.

We could continue to indefinitely point out the contrasts in this land of hope for a few, but of pain for many.

DECADES OF DICTATORSHIP

I know that you are aware of the countless decades in which some Central American countries have known only dictatorship. How very difficult it is to ask freedom to walk along lands which, for so many generations, have been planted with the seeds of injustice! I ask you, dear friends, what alternative is there to freedom? Has one dictator who replaced another at any moment overcome his fear of freedom? Have the imprisoned been freed because a tyrant has changed ideology or

◼ Anastasio Somoza Debayle.

name? Have a mother's tears stopped flowing because a tyrant of the left replaced one of the right, or because one of the right replaced one of the left? It is simply another mother who now weeps. We know that no political ideology can justify destruction. We know all too well that when one mother cries, her tears join those of many others.

The Central American crisis is not a new one: its roots are embedded in a history of unjust structures, of bitter political, social, and economic realities, and of the continuing presence of foreign interests within the region.

North-South and East-West problems intersect over Central America. Sombre forebodings radiate from where they cross. While some believe that this cross must be destroyed by combating social injustices and resuming the road to economic growth, others believe it will only be dismantled when the horizontal line of the East-West ideological confrontation is destroyed. While this debate continues, Central America grows poorer. Its economies stagnate, spreading poverty even more. Its guerrilla movements, of one or another ideology, continue, perpetuate death and desolation.

The Government of the United States has declared that it considers the Sandinista leaders of Nicaragua a Marxist threat which could expand north, through Mexico, to its own borders, and south, through Costa Rica, to the Panama Canal. It has also declared that the guerrilla movement in El Salvador is sustained by military aid and support proceeding from Cuba through Nicaragua. If we add to these declarations those made by the Soviet Union, Cuba, and Nicaragua, it becomes obvious that embedded in the already grave Central American problems that exist within the North-South context is a significant East-West component.

THE THREAT OF TOTAL WAR IN CENTRAL AMERICA

Tensions between the countries of the region have been sharpened by the participation of extra-regional actors. The presence of these actors aggravates the conflict to the level of an ideological confrontation.

In the past, the most decisive influence was

exerted by the United States. With its present foreign policy, the United States seems to indicate that it intends to maintain its hegemony over the Central American region. This objective is challenged by the support given by the Socialist bloc to the Salvadoran guerrillas, the Guatemalan guerrilla movement, and the Sandinista government of Nicaragua.

Whatever the focus used in the analysis of Central America, the threat of war is an imminent possibility. This increases political and economic uncertainty. While it is now possible to speak of controlled military expenditures in some Latin American countries, the arms race continues to be forced upon most countries of Central America. Some countries suffer from the burdens imposed by guerrilla warfare, which is found, at least partially, within the context of the East-West confrontation.

The covert or public provision of arms by extra-regional powers to some countries of the area drags us irretrievably to a confrontation. We will soon reach a point of no return in which ultimately war will reign. The paths of war can only mean a bleaker future for Central America: one that is reft with poverty and oppression.

DIGNITY AND DECORUM

When the democracies of the world fail to use their own tools of dialogue and persuasion to fight for freedom, they defer to tyrants and oppressors. We must work with political integrity to gain respect for the self-determination of nations, for the freedom of peoples and their right to exercise their democratic privileges.

While some talk about disarmament, nuclear warheads are lifted into space and lowered into the depths of oceans. They now threaten us from where they are least expected. I am afraid to think, not only of the proliferation of these tools of destruction, but also of how some men appear to have taken leave of their senses, to have lost their souls, and forgotten the ideals of humanity. God forbid that cynicism about disarmament should reach a point where treaties are unscrupulously signed to eliminate weapons which are already obsolete, while we continue racing even faster toward death and destruction. In Central America, we speak of peace even as arms are distributed to our young.

These are sad years for the cause of freedom in the Americas! The heartrending scream of trampled rights can be heard throughout the continent. There are those who have come to power only to claim that mothers should not lament the death of a son, or a friend the torture of his brother. The most atrocious crimes are committed in the name of freedom. In the name of freedom, the tyrants of Latin America have expelled men and women from their lands after persecuting their families and peers. This time no pity will be shown to the people who choose the path of war. He who encourages war in his heart, he who encourages it with money, will end up, blinded, sending his own children to die in it. The fear of freedom causes many to seek refuge in arms. The fear of dialogue makes some seek protection in dogmatism. We cannot turn our back on history. How often have we conquered one hatred only to succumb to another! How many times has democracy been threatened by the plots of disloyal armed forces!

At times it would seem that the world is not concerned with the atrocities that occur within the borders of other nations. The leader who

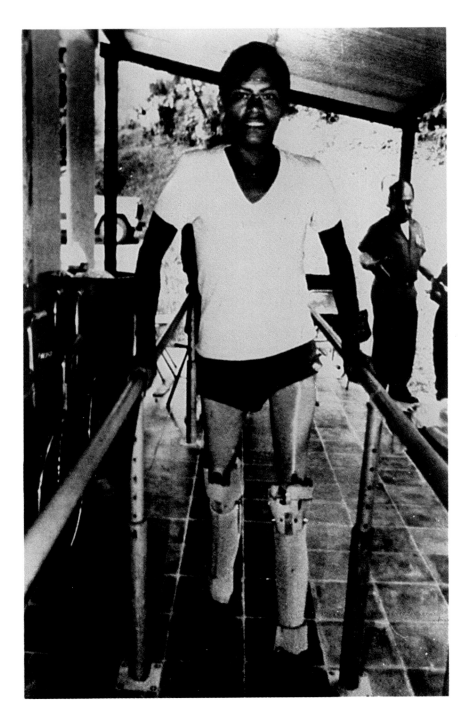

tramples men because of the colour of their skin, or who persecutes and imprisons them because they scream of their poverty or cry of their hunger, is received with the same honours given to the leader who has been freely elected and governs for the benefit of the majority of his people, with respect for all of their rights. How often the tyrant sits at the same table with the liberator! How often a powerful government gives better treatment to the leader who withholds freedoms than to the one who governs in the name of his people!

MAY NO ONE SEEK REFUGE IN WAR

Some say that the battle for peace in Central America must be won in Washington. Others say that the battle for Washington must be won in Central America. I assert that the battle for Washington should be won there, with paths chosen by the people of North America. The battle for peace in Central America should be won here, with paths chosen by Central Americans.

The Organization of American States will belong to George Washington and Simón Bolívar on the day when the representative of a tyrant is not found here, on the day when only ambassadors who reflect the free expression of each and every one of the peoples of the Americas gather here.

Let us not mistake the facts. May no one seek refuge in war. May no one fear freedom. Let us work together for democracy and freedom for all Americans.

PEACE AS A PRIORITY

Pope John Paul II said: «the name of development is peace». Peace can exist without development, but development cannot exist without peace. Costa Rica is the best example of the fact that the conflict between totalitarianism and democracy is not resolved in the fields of battle, it is won on the terrain of ideas, of ethics, of solidarity, of justice, and of prosperity.

■ With Pope John Paul II and Margarita.

CONTADORA AND ITS SUPPORT GROUP

Central America is not alone in its struggle for peace. Over the past four years, the Contadora Group, though its mediation, has contributed to the peaceful resolution of conflicts. The Contadora and the Support Groups express the solidarity of sister states that, having again found the way to democracy, proclaim that freedom and democracy are essential for reconciliation in Central America. The Organization of American States has promised to assist in this effort to achieve peace and democracy by monitoring commitments made by its members. The United Nations has been closely interested in the problem of Central America pursuant to its responsibilities of promoting peace throughout the world.

Contadora has not died. Costa Rica will continue to support its efforts as long as a whisper of hope exists. We desire a peace and we appeal to reason.

■ The representatives of Contadora and its support group meet.

We possess a tradition of freedom which calls us to serve as its responsible and conscientious advocates. If we turn our backs on this tradition, the tragedy of war will overtake us and we will be among its many victims.

In Managua with Daniel Ortega. Behind and to the right, the Nicaraguan Ambassador to Costa Rica, Claudia Chamorro.

ALONG THE PATHS OF PEACE

AN ALLIANCE FOR FREEDOM AND DEMOCRACY

Costa Rica believes in the necessity of an alliance for freedom and democracy in the Americas. We will not ally ourselves either economically or politically with governments that oppress their peoples.

I call for an alliance for freedom and democracy in the Americas and the Caribbean: freedom and democracy for development, freedom and democracy for justice, freedom and democracy for peace.

In San Isidro de Coronado, accompanied by Ministers Hernán Garrón and Rodrigo Arias.

In this magnificent political undertaking there is no room for the cowardly or for the weak-spirited. It is time to respond to the challenge and make aspirations realities. It is time for those of us who believe that freedom and democracy are the only arms for overcoming injustice to close ranks and unite.

A GLIMPSE OF THE FUTURE

Although times are difficult and the threats to our peace are overwhelming, I am confident that peace will endure and even flourish. My confidence rests, not only on the strength of our history, but also in your relentless struggle to defend the most sacred of ideals. Together we will find an end to the violence that threatens us.

We have the right to fight beyond our borders when the weapon employed is dialogue. That right exists when we seek peace among men, when we aspire to freedom for everyone, when we propagate the supremacy of love over hate.

Not only will you witness how peace can be strengthened during these difficult times; you

■ The people of Costa Rica have always cradled the concept of peace.

will also be the protagonists of that struggle. To its youth, Costa Rica owes the preservation and safety of its treasured peace. We know that we will fulfil our duty to them with a humility that accompanies only the greatest causes.

Today, Costa Rica has set its sights on its young citizens. The strength of change and the purity of the ideals that must inspire us at this time are

in the hands of our youth.

We do not want the young people of our country or any other nation to be soldiers of death. Every young person should be an apostle of freedom and of progress.

The youth of the Americas must look to the future and reject the bitterness planted by fanatical and self-centred ideologies. The promise of

progress that tempts us to renounce freedom will never materialize. Peace that is maintained by cannons will never be true peace.

ESQUIPULAS I

Because in Costa Rica we do not know the fear of liberty, we will not abandon our faith in dialogue. That is why we went to the «Meeting of the Central American Presidents» in Esquipulas, Guatemala. In Esquipulas, Central America reaffirmed its faith in democracy and in freedom. The government of Managua was cautioned that only democracy can shield us against the suffering and war we wish to avoid.

A TIME FOR PEACE

Peace in the Americas can only be maintained through the independence of each one of its nations, through political and economic cooperation among its peoples, through the enjoyment of the broadest liberties, through the validity of stable democratic regimes, through the fulfilment of its citizens' basic needs, and through progressive disarmament.

Peace demands its time. The dictatorships which for so many years have ruled the destiny of many people of this continent, have systematically violated human rights and have submitted populations to poverty, exploitation, servitude, inequality, and injustice.

Peace demands its time. In a few countries of the Americas, dictatorships persist, and with them survives a disregard for the highest of human values. The peace that demands its time also demands an end to existing dictatorships. It is imperative that all of us together call for the removal of such tyrannies where people are the victims of the absence of freedom. Such a tran-

■ With Fidel Castro.

sition toward democracy should occur, preferably, without bloodshed.

The peace that demands its time demands an end to extreme poverty and the establishment of genuine equality for all. Without this commitment to justice, conflicts will persist.

The peace that demands its time demands the strengthening of democracy in all the nations of the Americas. Where the doors of freedom and democracy have been opened, where all men may freely and periodically elect their rulers, where political pluralism prevails, as well as dialogue and the free expression of ideas, armed conflict can only be interpreted as the desire to establish a new dictatorship: it cannot be regarded as the struggle for freedom, but rather as the conflict of fanatics who try to forcefully impose the ideas of a minority.

IN SEARCH OF SUPPORT

I ask the world to understand. I ask the great powers of all ideologies to understand that to make a pact for democracy in the Americas, for pluralism and for freedom, is to help mankind and promote peace.

As we face the adversities of these five years, the dangers that multiply in the Central American isthmus, the increasing inequalities, Costa Rica renews its unwavering faith in the superior destiny of man, because the soul of the people is nourished by freedom, democracy, and peace.

We are hopeful that, above all, the return of political democracy in the Americas may be accompanied by a more equitable international economic order.

In the recent past of Latin America, we have seen how efficient and expert bankers stimulated the dreams of greatness of generals who restrained rights and liberties in many lands. Yesterday, international banks competed fiercely to lend to tyrants. Today, they unite to collect from democracies. Yesterday, they cared little that their money maintained the rule of despots. Today, they are not concerned with the suffering of those who pay in liberty. No one has the right to invoke the «apolitical» in order to commit the amoral. Such an attitude damages the dignity of our shared humanity and endangers the civilized basis of international relations.

We have made the world smaller. Let us extend our vision beyond that of the banks to the strug

gles for peace and liberty. Let us reassert their value in defeating poverty, in guaranteeing respect for human rights in every corner of the globe. Many are the noble causes that have been debased under the scrutiny of the financier. Let us respond again to those noble efforts in order to perceive the world anew. Let us not fear the only vision that can lead us to a durable and secure peace, to a world that struggles together in solidarity to free itself from misery.

A historic visit to the United Nations. Costa Rican efforts for peace in Central America received worldwide support.

▶

■ A greeting from Colombian President Belisario Betancur.

■ Theodore Schultz, Nobel Laureate in Economics.

48

A few days ago, I proposed a peace plan for our part of the world. I believe that if we speak of putting an end to war, we should do so today. If we propose that dialogue replace the rifle, we should dialogue today.

We want time-limits for the fulfilment of commitments. As democrats, we want the agreements achieved through dialogue to become realities. We no longer want to hear the sound of a rifle or see the sad pilgrimage of those who are forced to flee their lands. We cannot observe with indifference the pain of those who cannot freely express their ideas.

To many it may seem that the cry of Costa Rica is a romantic cry. My first months as President have taught me that it is time to cry out if to do so is to struggle for peace, if to do so is to defend the poor.

The commitment of the Western world to strengthen democracy in all of our countries must prevail over any political or economic condition that might interfere in the democratic process of the Americas. In the Americas, peace should be democratic, pluralistic, tolerant, free. Peace will be impossible as long as dogmatism and intransigence obstruct dialogue. To work together for democracy, freedom and development, is to work together for peace.

The struggle for peace in Central America is the historic struggle of all democracies. Now, as never before, the time has come for the people of the United States and of Costa Rica to recognize their shared principles and values.

The history of Central America is a heartrending one. In the past few years, over one million persons have lost their homes. More than one hundred thousand have died. If we were to engrave their names on a wall, as the names of those who died in Vietnam are engraved here in Washington, we would have to build a wall twice as long to inscribe all of the Central Americans who have fallen victim to violence in these years.

■ In the White House with President Ronald Reagan,
Secretary of State George Shultz, and Foreign Minister of
Costa Rica Rodrigo Madrigal Nieto.

Being congratulated by Richard Hunt, Marshall of Harvard University, while receiving a Doctorate Honoris Causa in Law.

I have come to Mexico with the same message that many thousands of my compatriots have shared with these lands: a liberating message of democracy and peace. I have come to expand the ties of friendship that join our nations. They are ties born of the special culture that we share, the pride of Latin America, ties that have been zealously preserved, in the history of our nations, by artists, teachers, poets, workers and politicians.

I have come with the moral authority of the oldest democracy in Latin America. I have come to ask you to share proudly the values that are dear to us both. I have come to request that strength of the Spain of yesterday and of today, to attain the peace, liberty, and democracy of Central America. I have come to ask for the strength of Spain so that we can share the visionary courage that will make the economic development of my nation more secure.

Of the triumphant Spain, we ask for the support of our endeavours in order for peace, an authentic and fruitful peace that permits the integral development of the human being, to triumph in Central America as well.

■ Miguel de la Madrid, President of Mexico, expressing his support for Costa Rica's peace efforts.

With the King and Queen of Spain.

With His Royal Highness Don Felipe upon receiving the Prince of Asturias Prize.

Peace must come to Central America by the path of democracy. The peoples of Central America cannot permit cannons to continue threatening justice and development. Yet we do not want the return of the bitter and sterile peace offered by dictatorships, whatever their ideological labels. Peace and democracy are inseparable concepts: the first emerges from the second.

My faith grows when I see that Spain supports the cause for peace and democracy in Central America. United, Spain and Costa Rica declare: «Enough of the fear which withholds freedom from the people! Enough of the fear which threatens peace!»

On this occasion I greet the noble and cultured people of England, that crib of great men, architects of the heroic deeds which transformed the

During a visit to the Capitol in September, 1987. On the left, Congressman Thomas Foley; on the right, Jim Wright, Speaker of the House.

■ Delivering
the
commencement
speech
at Harvard.

55

course of history. Great Britain and Costa Rica base their lifestyles on the purest of democratic traditions. They coincide in their fundamental values and aspiration to higher goals. Those traditions and values have made them strong, even through the most difficult circumstances.

With Margarita, Her Majesty the Queen, Elizabeth II, and Prince Philip, Duke of Edinburgh, in Buckingham Palace.

■ At 10
Downing
Street,
London, with
Prime
Minister
Margaret
Thatcher.

It is not a coincidence that Germany welcomes us with open arms. This Germany,which shed the blood of many sons, values our peace. It was Germany that , after a hecatomb, has contributed so generously to promote development in the Third World, understands our needs.

I have come to ask for the support of Germany in this task which is as urgent as it is mutual: the struggle for peace through peaceful methods. I am convinced that the success of this undertaking will represent a triumph for the civilized world.

Many coincidences and similarities link us to the nations of the European Economic Community. Costa Rica rejects violence and war as a means to overcome political conflict. Our peaceful society is ready to prevent foreign hegemonic forces from involving it in conflict against its spirit, its interests, and its will.

We have committed ourselves to the struggle for the pre-eminence of democracy, for the dignity of the individual, and for the respect of human rights. These values are widely recognized by the peoples of Europe who saw the birth of the democratic system within their lands. My country has had to live through a difficult time in its history: through an economic recession which threatens the social stability we value so much.

In the last few years, we have witnessed the intensification of European aid to our region. It has transcended mere promises and become a

In Bonn, with Chancellor Helmut Kohl.

tangible reality. We are confident that this aid will increase in the future, following the agreements reached in San José, and will acquire increasingly greater effectiveness in projects supporting the development of my country and that of Central America.

Costa Rica and France know that only with strong democracies and just economies will freedom defeat fear and renew the creative spirit of all human beings.

Costa Rica's need for international aid to achieve economic development is not insignificant. Our will is focused on the supreme effort to reactivate and modernize our national apparatus of production.

59

From the Reichstag in West Berlin, President Arias and his wife Margarita survey the Berlin Wall, with Hans Jürgen, Administrative Chief of the Bundestag. The Costa Rican President predicted at the Inter-American Summit held in San José on 28 October 1989: "We will see a world with a Europe that will achieve unprecedented political and economic unity, where the Berlin Wall will fall and where there will no longer be some Europeans who are poor and others who are rich, some who are prisoners and others who are free." A few weeks later the Berlin Wall fell, forever.

Together with François Mitterand, President of the French Republic.

We need peace to reactivate our economies and the Central American Common Market, which was, until recent years, an important source of support for commercial exchange. We need peace to encourage investment and generate employment. We need peace to permit the many thousands of Central American refugees to return to their homes and jobs. We need peace to allow us to continue in the construction of societies that are more developed, more just and more free. We need peace to re-establish harmony and fraternity among our nations.

61

In Paris, with Prime Minister of France, Jacques Chirac.

With Mikhail Gorbachev.

THE GUATEMALA AGREEMENT

The five Central American Presidents.

■ The Presidents Daniel Ortega of Nicaragua, José Napoleón Duarte of
El Salvador, Marco Vinicio Cerezo of Guatemala, José Azcona Hoyo
of Honduras, and Oscar Arias of Costa Rica sign the Central American Peace Plan.

ESQUIPULAS II

IN FRONT THE NATIONAL PALACE

O
n 7 August 1987, each of the five Presidents of Central America crossed the cobblestone plaza in front of Guatemala's National Palace. I am sure that each of us meditated on the peace agreement which we were going to endorse. To one side, an Indian woman holding her child to her breast watched us go by. Her hair braided and her feet bare, she personified the air of resignation that has characterized Central Americans for decades. Her face was marked with sadness; she had witnessed far too much violence.

After signing the Peace Plan in Guatemala, the

five Presidents left the National Palace and crossed the cobblestone plaza. The Indian woman approached me with her child in her arms and said: «Thank you, Señor Presidente, for this son and for the one who is fighting». That moment reaffirmed my belief that I should continue working for peace in Central America. That is my commitment to that woman and to 27 million Central Americans.

I SHALL CONTINUE DREAMING

I cannot promise you, as I depart for the meeting of Presidents, that we will triumph. What I can do is assure you that we will never be defeated. I do not walk alone. I do not travel a path forged by vain purposes. I am faithful to a mandate; faithful to a nation that entrusted me with its dreams and which demands that I carry them into the future, delivering them to a posterity unblemished.

We are going to Guatemala to speak of peace. The entire world will speak of the peace of Central America. A few months ago, people

With Presidents Cerezo of Guatemala an Duarte of El Salvador, an the Costa Rican Foreig Minister Rodrigo Madrigal Nieto.

spoke only of war in the region. We are going to speak of the peace proposed by Costa Rica. As I have said to you many times, our peace is based on the values of democracy and freedom upheld by the Costa Rican people. We want to share what we have.

You exist, Costa Rica, despite all of the sorrow and all of the threats. Many have tried to tell you that your existence is an impossible one, that you are a fiction, that you cannot continue to be different, that the world's dreams have come to an end, that you must take up arms and form an army. They wish to call you a coward when your courage rests in choosing not to bear arms. They say that you should be realistic and allow your children to participate in foreign wars. They want you to proclaim you are free, yet try to force you to think in their limited terms. They tell you that you should be black or white. They try to convince you that some say all truth and others all lies.

Today I say to Costa Rica that more than a few will discourage our efforts for peace. Some long for violence to resolve conflicts. Those minorities will be unable to disturb the endeavours of a

people united in a history of peace and committed to a free future.

There are those who speak of the successes or failures of the Peace Plan. Perhaps they do not fully understand its meaning, the nature of our purpose, and the objectives of our enterprise. The Peace Plan is a constant dialogue, an evolutionary process, vigorous and unstoppable, which overcomes each obstacle on our way to peace. This dialogue gains force every moment, because every moment more men and women hold steadfastly to its message of hope.

Every time we stumble, every time we are delayed, there are those who claim we have failed. Imagine if that were the case with the great decisions of our lives. How many of us, upon failing at a task on one day, have been forced to complete it that same day? If that were the case, we wouldn't be here today. It is absurd to try and deny men and nations the right to overcome, to rectify, to make another attempt! We say to those who see failure in every fall that to ensure peace it is necessary to fight for it daily. We will do so.

I will keep dreaming. Costa Rica will keep

dreaming. Peace can never be a mistake, for dialogue will never be the banner of fanatics. There are battles that will be won always in life and in death, like those won by Cid Campeador. They are the battles for the freedom of man. They are the battles that, as I have repeated a thousand times, do not know defeat.

In my struggle for the peace of Central America, I have been the servant of my people's will. Like all of you, I am the brother of those dreams that were forged by our ancestors in the mountains, valleys and seas of this land. With the strength of the peace we have inherited, we will force the threat of war to retreat from our borders.

There is a greater chance for peace in Central America than ever before. There is a greater chance for democracy in Latin America than ever before. Working in liberty we have the opportunity to defeat poverty. We shall not allow poverty to continue to exist, strengthenece by dictatorship.

The obstacles in the way of peace, in its reconciliatory efforts, have cost Central America and the world much bloodshed and many frustrations. Let us pray that the pact for peace which

we have just signed does not meet with the same fate. Let us work, like never before, to make this pact a reality. Let us learn to struggle firmly, but calmly, against those who fear peace, those who seek refuge in war, those who have lost faith, those who have forgotten mercy.

Let us say to all of those men of the Americas who were forced to abandon their native lands that they must not lose hope. The painful prayer of the wandering Central American family must end with a return to its native land and a reunion with freedom. Their return must coincide with the silencing of rifles. It must coincide with the opening of prison gates to liberate innocent men. It must coincide with the free and fearless discussion of all ideas, and with the abandonment of violence as the weapon of political struggle.

We must fight so that Central Americans can again lift their heads and look to the future with optimism.

Satisfied with the advances of the Peace Plan, the five Central American presidents meet in Guatemala.

■ In New York, with Javier Pérez de Cuéllar, Secretary
General of the United Nations, José Sarney, President of
Brazil, and Mario Soares, President of Portugal.

NATIONAL AND INTERNATIONAL SUPPORT

OUR ALLIANCES

In these coming years we must succeed in the noble causes we share. In these causes you will be soldiers and judges of the duties of those who govern. Let us share the journey and enjoy together the success of our endeavours for more peace, for more liberty, for more democracy.

Let us work together for that freedom without names and without dogmas, for that unique and noble democracy which we know so well. How sad it is to see that freedom, for which so many have died, has ploughs to fill the land because all the iron has being used to make chains that the imprison so many people.

Before the United States House of Representatives when he spoke the famous words: "Give peace a chance".

Our alliances must be closer and stronger than ever. We cannot take one step back on the road we have taken toward peace! May political prisoners never return to the gaols they were freed from! Let us struggle together for the release of those who unjustly remain in those jails. May no newspaper be closed. May no radio station be silenced. Let us struggle together for the opening of other newspapers, radio transmitters and television networks. May no dictator return to power where a leader has been freely elected. Let us work together to be rid of the tyrannies that persist in the Americas.

A CHANCE FOR PEACE

Give peace a chance. Let us not allow the fear of some and blindness of others to prevail. If we work together, we will achieve peace. It will be difficult. But has progress ever been easy? Here in the United States it was a hard-won struggle to wrest a living from the land, to win equality for all people, to preserve freedom, and to travel into outer space itself! Yet the more difficult the obstacle, the greater the satisfaction in overcoming it.

It is difficult to understand why a climate of agreement has not been reached in our bloody Central America. I have often asked myself why wounds remain open when their pain is so great; why intransigence flourishes when we long for

dialogue; why war does not cease when reconciliation can no longer be postponed; why the same people who cry out for peace, beat the drums of war; why we are so quick to conspire for death and so slow to negotiate.

There is no peace because there is no reconciliation. There is no reconciliation because there is no justice. There is no justice because there is no mercy. There is no mercy because there is no love.

The countries of Europe cannot be content with the stability of their own democracies. Europe must cooperate in the consolidation and development of the democratic process in Latin America. This requires a great effort: the condemnation of all forms of authoritarianism, the demand for the respect of human rights and democratization as prerequisites for international cooperation.

Today a new climate is evolving in Central America. A lost faith is being reborn. We must aid its growth. We must believe again in freedom, in dialogue, in the free expression of the will of the majority. I have come to ask you to share in our undertaking. I have come to request your help.

The Costa Rican delegation to this Organization will present to the Assembly the Peace Plan signed in Guatemala. We will ask for its approval as a resolution of the United Nations and for its adoption by this Assembly. We will ask that it be backed by the full political power with which the nations of the world create and support just causes here in this forum. I am certain that we will receive this support. I am certain that together we can say that the power of

President Arias with President Ronald Reagan during a meeting at the White House. Representing Costa Rica: are, Rodrigo Madrigal Nieto, Foreign Minister; Guido Fernández, Ambassador to the United States; Fernando Volio, President of the Legislative Assembly; and John Biehl, Adviser to President Arias. Representing the United States: Frank Carlucci, Secretary of Defense; Elliot Abrams, Assistant Secretary for Inter-American Affairs; José Sorzano, Advisor to President Reagan for Latin America; Howard Baker, Chief of Staff; John Whitehead, Deputy Secretary of State, and George Bush, Vice President.

diplomacy and the validity of political accords undertaken in good faith will always be more effective than weapons, that they will be stronger than war. I am certain that we will walk the path of peace together in order to banish war from our region once and for all.

The French historian and statesman, François Guizot, said: «Pessimists are merely onlookers: it is the optimists who change the world». I have come to invite you to participate with great optimism in this struggle to establish in Central America a territory of freedom, justice and peace.

I recognize that the forces we must defeat are powerful. I recognize that it is easier to predict destruction. I also recognize that anyone can cause destruction. In one day, the most beautiful of cities can be destroyed. In one day, war can erupt. In one day, thousands upon thousands of men and women can lose their possessions. In one day, thousands of children condemned to hunger are born in the world. Anyone can be part of the irresponsibility of one day.

The life of the person who destroys is easy. He can be stupid, ignorant and lazy. He can be

Guatemalan school children express their joy after the signing of the Peace Plan.

weak, selfish and insensitive. He can find refuge in fanaticism, cast the traitorous stone, and even justify violence to give free reign to his hatred and frustration. On the other hand, the person who builds, who assumes responsibility for the future, who is willing to share the possibility of preserving peace and decreasing injustice, must be ruled by the norms of love, discipline and wisdom.

Some fear the peace accord signed by the Central Americans. They say that what we want to achieve in Central America has never been

In Washington, with Elliot Abrams, Assistant Secretary for Inter-America Affairs and George Shult Secretary of State.

At a dinner in New York, with Javier Pérez de Cuéllar, Secretary General of the United Nations, his wife Marcela, and John Silver, President of Boston University.

done. They say that dialogue is impractical where hatred is so deep-rooted. They say that reconciliation is impossible when differences have been so pronounced over so many years. They say it is impossible to walk side by side when such extreme ideologies divide our peoples. They say that the word of one who has lied can never be trusted.

I say that is not true. It is our duty to attempt something different. We cannot renounce imagination and courage to promote the changes demanded by society. We cannot continue walking blindly through history, burdened by poverty and tormented by war. We cannot grope through the new path, stumbling, waiting for others to guide us. We say peace; we say democracy; we say freedom; because we know how far we want to go, because we know what the future we want to build is like. We are tired of shedding tears. We long to find shared ideals to work together for development. We want to take the destiny of our region into our own hands.

■ Philip Habib, special envoy of President Ronald Reagan, meets with President Arias in San José.

■ With Christopher Dodd, Democratic Senator from Connecticut in the Presidential Office in San José.

COMMITMENTS

The signated hour is at hand; the hour that Bolívar proclaimed. It is time to choose between weapons and freedom, between arms build-up and development, between inequality and justice. History has proven that these roads are exclusive. We have had enough of armed forces that subjugate their nations and frighten their citizens. The only armed men that the Americas can tolerate are those who are faithful to the Constitution and the Law, faithful to their people.

The principles that led us to sign the agreement in Guatemala have forced us to travel the path to peace, despite its barren terrain. We will continue to build bridges, regardless of the storms that occasionally assault us. Every step forward brings a new hope for peace to more Central Americans; it is reassuring when we go two steps forward for every step back. Every day more men and women leave their weapons in order to grasp the tools of labour and help in the construction of the paths of peace.

Costa Rica is the unarmed camp of Central

America. We ask for peace and respect for human rights. We have rejected the appeal of those who incite us to hate, of those who would

like us to see the world in terms of black and white. Freedom can have many colours. We need not fear it.

We have asked for the silencing of guns so that men might speak to one another. Today there are 27 million human beings living in Central America. We can no longer live as we did yesterday. In Central America no plantation can ever again justify oppression for the profit of a few. The region has five nations whose peoples want to be free and who justifiably demand their right to a shared and equitable development.

Costa Rica's Peace Plan, accepted by Central America on the seventh of August, proclaims that further violence is unnecessary to achieve freedom. Those who persist in trusting arms alone will sooner or later lose their own children in the old, cruel game whose first rule is: «He who lives by the sword will die by the sword». No one should lie to himself. Those who preach war as the only course of action must be prepared to send their own children to fight it and not pay for the children of others to die in senseless conflict.

◀ In Bonn with Foreign Minister Hans Dietrich Genscher.

■ President Arias converses with Prime Minister Itzhak Shamir from Israel in the library of his home.

◀ With Joao Clemente Baena Suarez, Secretary General of the Organization of American States.

THE NOBEL PEACE PRIZE

Egil Aarvik, Nobel Peace Committee Chairman, during the Nobel Peace Prize ceremony.

PEACE HAS NO FINISHING LINE

In Oslo, the President shows the Nobel Prize medal to his wife, Margarita.

When you chose to honour me with this prize, you chose to honour my land of peace: you chose to honour Costa Rica. When, in this year of 1987, you fulfilled the wish of Alfred E. Nobel to encourage the efforts for peace in the world, you chose to encourage the efforts to secure peace in Central America. I am most grateful for this recognition of our search for peace. All of us in Central America are grateful.

No one knows better than the honourable members of this Committee, that this Prize symbolizes your wish to promote the initiative for peace in Central America. With your decision, you are contributing to its success; you are declaring

President Arias makes his speech in the Great Hall of the University of Oslo after receiving the 1987 Nobel Peace Prize.

In Oslo, with Gro Harlem Brundland, Prime Minister of Norway, and Rodrigo Arias Sánchez, Minister of the Presidency of Costa Rica.

that you know that the search for peace can never end, that it is a permanent cause which needs the support of genuine friends, of people with the courage to promote change toward peace despite all obstacles.

Peace is not a matter of prizes or of trophies. It is not the product of a victory nor of a command. It has no borders, no time-limits, nothing fixed in the definition of its achievements.

Peace is a never-ending process; it is the result of innumerable decisions made by many persons in many lands. It is an attitude, a way of life, a way of solving problems and of resolving conflicts. It cannot be forced on the smallest nation, nor can it be imposed by the most powerful. It can neither ignore our differences nor overlook our common interests. It requires us to work and live together.

Peace is not only a matter of noble words and Nobel lectures. We already have an abundance of words, glorious words, inscribed in the declarations of the United Nations, the World Court, the Organization of American States and a network of international treaties and laws. We need deeds which respect these words, which

■ In Oslo, President Arias with his mother Lillyam, his wife Margarita, his children Sylvia Eugenia and Oscar Felipe, his sister Cecilia, and his brother-in-law, Miguel Angel González.

honour the commitments avowed in these laws. We need to strengthen our institutions of peace, such as the United Nations, to ensure that they are used on behalf of the weak as well as the strong.

I give no heed to those who doubt, nor to those who want to deny that a lasting peace can be truly accepted by those marching under different ideological banners, not to those who are more accustomed to cannons of war than to treaties of peace.

In Central America, we do not seek solely peace, nor solely a peace to be followed one day by political progress. Instead we seek peace and democracy together, indivisible: an end to the shedding of human blood which is inseparable from an end to the violation of human rights. We do not judge, much less condemn, the political or ideological system of any nation which is freely chosen and not exported. We cannot impose on sovereign states models of government which they themselves have not chosen. But we can and do insist that every government respect universal human rights, whose value transcends all national borders and ideological labels. We believe that justice and peace can only prosper together, never apart. A nation which mistreats its own citizens is more likely to mistreat its neighbours.

Receiving the Nobel Peace Prize on the tenth of December is a wonderful coincidence for me. My son, Oscar Felipe, present here, is eight years old today. I say to him, and through him to all the children of my country, that we must never resort to violence, that we must never support military solutions to the problems of Central America. For the sake of the new generation, we must emphasize that today, more than ever, peace can only be achieved with its own instruments: dialogue and understanding, tolerance and forgiveness, freedom and democracy.

I know that you join us in our call to the members of the international community, and in particular to those nations of East and West, which have much more power and resources than my small nation can ever hope to wield. To them I say with the greatest urgency: let Central Americans decide the future of Central America. Leave the interpretation of and the compliance with the Peace Plan to us. Support the efforts

■ With Oscar Felipe, Margarita and Sylvia Eugenia.

■ Oscar Felipe, representative of all of the children in Costa Rica.

for peace in our region, not the forces of war; send us not swords but ploughshares, not spears but pruning hooks. If, for your own purposes, you cannot stop hoarding the weapons of war, then, in the name of God, at least leave us in peace.

I say here, to His Royal Majesty, to the honourable members of the Nobel Peace Prize Committee, and to the wonderful people of Norway, that I accept this prize because I know how passionately you share our search for peace and our hope for success. If, in the coming years, peace prevails, eliminating violence and war, a great measure of this peace will be owed to the faith of the Norwegian people and will be to your credit forever.

■ With his friend John H. Biehl
on the day of the
Nobel Peace Prize ceremony.

■ With Willy Brandt and Carlos Andrés Pérez in Oslo.

■ His son, Oscar Felipe, looking at the Nobel Prize medal.

DEN NORSKE NOBELKOMITÉ

HAR OVERENSSTEMMENDE MED REGLENE I DET AV

ALFRED NOBEL

DEN 27. NOVEMBER 1895 OPPRETTEDE TESTAMENTE TILDELT

OSCAR ARIAS SÁNCHEZ

NOBELS FREDSPRIS FOR 1987

OSLO, 10. DESEMBER 1987

President Arias shows the Nobel Prize certificate to his children Sylvia Eugenia and Oscar Felipe. His mother, Lillyam, observes the medal.

After giving a lecture in the Great Hall at the University of Oslo, the day after receiving the Nobel Peace Prize.

ONLY PEACE CAN WRITE THE NEW HISTORY

With Margarita, Prime Minister Brian Mulroney, the Costa Rican Ambassador to Canada, Dr. Marco Aurelio Guillén, and his wife Ileana.

YEARNING FOR PEACE

Peace consists, mainly, of the act of desiring it with all one's soul. This teachings of Erasmus are lived by the inhabitants of my small Costa Rica. Mine is a people whose children have never seen a combat plane, or a tank, or a battleship. One of my guests at this ceremony is Mr. José Figueres Ferrer. He is the man of vision who in 1948 abolished my homeland this army and thus set our history on a different course.

I COME FROM LATIN AMERICA

I do not receive this prize as Oscar Arias. Nor do I receive it as President of my country. I do not vainly claim to represent anyone or anything, but I do not fear the humility which identifies me with the great causes shared by all. I receive it as one of four hundred million Latin Americans, who seek — through the return of freedom and democracy— the way to overcome tremendous misery and injustice.

I am from that Latin America whose face is deeply scarred by tremendous pains by exile, torture, prison, and death of many of her men and women. I am from that Latin America which still suffers the burden of shameful totalitarian regimes.

THE SCARS OF THE AMERICAS

America is marked by deep scars. In the very years that she is seeking a return to freedom, the advent of democracy is revealing, for the first

■ King Olav V of Norway expresses his congratulations.

time, the horrible trail of torture, exile and death left by dictators. America has enormous problems to overcome. The inheritance of an unjust past has been aggravated by the tragic actions of tyrants who caused external debt, social insensitivity, economic destruction, corruption, and many other evils in our societies. These evils are in plain view for anyone to see.

It is not surprising that, before the magnitude of the challenge, despair imprisons many. It is not surprising that the prophets of the Apocalypse abound, announcing the failure of the fight against poverty, proclaiming the imminent downfall of the democracies, predicting the ineffectiveness of all efforts for peace.

I do not share this defeatism. I do not agree that realists must tolerate poverty, violence, and hate. I do not believe that a hungry man who expresses his suffering should be treated as a subversive. I can never accept that the law be used to justify tragedy, that things must remain as they are, that we must abandon all thought of a different world. The law is the path of freedom and as such must offer equal opportunity for the development of all.

FREEDOM WORKS MIRACLES

Freedom works miracles. For free men everything is possible. A democratic and free America can overcome the challenges confronting us. When I assumed the Presidency of Costa Rica, I called for an alliance of freedom and democracy in the Americas. I said then, and I repeat today, that we cannot ally ourselves either politically or economically with governments that oppress their peoples. Latin America has never known a single war between two democracies. That is reason enough for every person of good faith, for every government with good intentions, to support the efforts to stamp out tyranny.

AMERICA IS IN HASTE

America is in haste to be free. All of America must be free.

I come from a world with great problems which are going to be overcome in freedom. I come from a world which is in haste because hunger makes haste. I come from a world where we are in haste to render the paths of freedom irreversible, and to frustrate every attempt at oppression. I come from a world in haste to detain the fire of the guerrilla and of the soldier; young people are dying, brothers are dying, and tomorrow no one will understand why. I come from a world in haste to open the prison doors and let out the prisoners, in place of opening them to usher in free men.

America is in haste for her freedom, haste for her democracy, and requires the understanding of the entire world to liberate herself from dictators and from misery.

I COME FROM CENTRAL AMERICA

I receive this prize as one of 27 million Central Americans. Behind the democratic awakening in Central America, lay over a hundred years of cruel dictators, of injustice, of generalized poverty. To live through another century of violence, or to achieve peace by overcoming the fear of freedom: this is the choice before my small America. Only peace can write the new history. In Central America we will not lose faith. We will rectify our history. How sad that many of us believe that peace is a dream, that justice is an utopia, that shared prosperity is impossible! How sad that in this world there are those who do not understand that, in the former plantations of Central America, nations today search for a better destiny for their peoples! How sad that some do not understand that Central America wants, not to prolong its past, but to write a new future of hope for the young and dignity for the old!

United States Ambassador to Costa Rica, Francis Mc Neil gives his book to President Arias.

At Harvard with the President of the University, Derek Bok, and with Michael Dukakis.

TURNING DREAMS INTO REALITIES

The Central American isthmus is an area of great contrasts, but also one of encouraging harmony. Millions of men and women share dreams of freedom and development. In some countries, these dreams are crumbling with the systematic violation of human rights. They are being shattered by fratricidal wars in the countryside and the cities. They are confronting poverty so extreme that it paralyzes the heart. Poets who are the pride of humanity know that millions and millions of their countrymen cannot read their work because so many men and women are illiterate. In this anguished strip of land, there are painters and sculptors who will be admired forever, but there are also dictators who, having offended the dearest values of humankind, will hold no place in our memory. Central America neither wants, nor can afford, to merely dream. History demands that our dreams become realities. Today, there is no time to lose. Today, we can take our destiny into our own hands. In these lands, home to the oldest and strongest democracy of Latin America —

With John Sununu, Chief of Staff. To the right, Brent Scowcroft, National Security Adviser to President Bush.

that of Costa Rica— and to the most merciless dictators, the democratic awakening demands a special loyalty to freedom.

As the dictators of yesterday sufficed only to engender misery and to cripple hope, how absurd it is to imagine curing the evils of a dictatorship of one extreme with a dictatorship of the other! In Central America no one has the right to fear freedom nor to preach absolute truth. All dogmas have the same flaw. All are enemies of human creativity. So said Pascal: «We know a great deal to make us sceptical. We know very little to make us dogmatic!»

History can only move toward freedom. History can only be inspired by justice. To march against the current of history is to follow the path of shame, of poverty, and of oppression. There is no revolution without freedom. All oppression is contrary to the human spirit.

■ Surrounded by Costa Rican students.

FREEDOM: A SHARE DESIRE

Central America is halted at a terrible crossroads. Faced with the agonizing problems of poverty, there are those who from the mountain or from the government call for dictators of new ideological creeds, ignoring the cry for freedom of so many generations. Next to the grave evils of generalized poverty, evils defined within the North-South context, the East-West conflict is brewing. Where the problems of poverty meet ideological struggle, the fear of freedom raises a cross of ill omen for Central America.

Let us make no mistake. The only answer for Central America, the only solution to her poverty, the only answer to her political challenges, is liberation from misery and fear. Those who claim to solve the evils of centuries with a single dogma will do nothing but exacerbate yesterday's problems.

For centuries, men and women have sought freedom in Central America. No one must betray this sacred alliance. To do so would condemn

our small America to another hundred years of horrifying oppression, to another hundred years of meaningless death, to another hundred years of struggle for freedom.

I COME FROM COSTA RICA

I receive this prize as one of the 2.7 million Costa Ricans. My people breathe their sacred freedom from the two oceans which are our frontiers to the East and West. To the South and North, Costa Rica has nearly always been bordered by dictators and hunger.

We are a people without arms and we are fighting to continue to be a people without hunger.

We are a symbol of peace for America; we want also to be a symbol of development. We intend to demonstrate that peace is both a requirement and a product of development.

■ The Dalai Lama and the Archbishop of San José, Monsignor Román Arrieta Villalobos.

A LAND OF TEACHERS

My land is a land of teachers. For this reason it is a land of peace. We discuss our successes and our failures alike in complete freedom.

Because mine is a land of teachers, we have closed the barracks: our children walk with books under their arms rather than guns on their shoulders. We believe in dialogue, in negotiation, in the search for consensus. We repudiate violence. Because mine is a land of teachers, we believe in convincing rather than vanquishing our adversaries.

We prefer to raise the fallen rather than to crush them, because we believe that no one possesses absolute truth. Because mine is a land of teachers, we seek an economy of cooperation in solidarity rather than one of competition to the death.

For 118 years, education in my country has been compulsory and free. Today every inhabitant is protected by medical attention, and public housing is a fundamental commitment of my government.

A NEW ECONOMY

While we rejoice in our achievements, we do not ignore our concerns or problems.

In these difficult times, we must be capable of establishing a new economy to resume growth. We have declared that we do not want an economy insensitive to domestic needs or to the demands of the poor. We have declared that we will not, in the name of economic growth, renounce our aspiration to create a more egalitarian society. Today our country has the lowest unemployment rate in the Western hemisphere. We want to be the first country in Latin America free of slums. We are convinced that a land free of slums will be a land free of hatred, where even the poorest peoples can enjoy the privilege of working freely for development.

■ President Arias receives a greeting from the Costa Rican people.

STRONGER THAN A THOUSAND ARMIES

In these bitter years for Central America, many in my homeland have feared that the sick and fanatical violence that pervades Central America would contaminate our Costa Rica. Some Costa Ricans have been impelled by this fear to propose that an army could keep violence outside our borders. What senseless weakness! These thoughts are worth less than the thirty pieces of silver given to Judas. The strength of Costa Rica, the force which makes her invincible to violence and more powerful than a thousand armies, is the force of freedom, of principles, of the great ideals of our civilization. When ideals are lived out in honesty, when freedom is not greeted by fear, we are invulnerable to totalitarian blows.

In Costa Rica, we know that only freedom enables all the inhabitants of a country to fully participate in the political system. Only freedom enables men to be tolerant. The painful wanderings of so many Cubans, Nicaraguans, Paraguayans, Chileans and others, unable to return to their own lands, are evidence to the senseless rule of dogmatism. Freedom has no surname; democracy has no colour. One recognizes them wherever they exist in the eyes of the people.

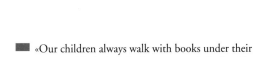

A PEACE PLAN

Faced with the proximity of violence in Central America, Costa Rica —her history and the idealism of her youth— enjoined me to bring to the battlefields of the region the peace of my people, the faith in dialogue, the need for tolerance. As the servant of my people, I proposed a peace plan for Central America. This plan is also based on the liberating call of Simón Bolívar, expressed in the tenacious and valiant work of the Contadora Group and the Support Group.

«Our children always walk with books under their arms, never with the barrel of a gun over their shoulders».

I AM ONE OF FIVE PRESIDENTS

I receive this prize as one of five Presidents, who before the entire world have made a pledge to our peoples to substitute a history of oppression for a future of freedom, to exchange a history of hunger for a posterity of progress, to change the weeping mothers and the violent death of youth for hope, for the path of peace which we wish to travel together.

Hope is the greatest force moving peoples. Hope transforms and creates new realities. It opens the way toward human freedom. To offer hope, courage must be joined to wisdom. Only then can we avoid violence; only then can we respond peacefully to offence.

However noble a cause may be, some will desire and promote its failure. Today there are some who seem to accept war as the normal course of affairs, as the way to solve problems. How ironic that powerful forces are irritated by the interruption of war —by the attempt to destroy reasons for hatred! How ironic that the attempt to stop war provokes anger and attacks, as if we

were disturbing a dream a necessary path, nor a heartrending evil! How ironic that the efforts for peace reveal those for whom hatred is stronger than love, in whom the longing for a military path to power destroys reason, overwhelms shame, and betrays history!

MAY ALL ARMS BE SILENCED

In Central America, we five Presidents have signed an accord to seek a firm and lasting peace. We seek that arms be silenced and men speak. Conventional arms are wounding our children; conventional arms are killing our youth.

The dread of nuclear war, the horrible depictions of an atomic apocalypse, seem to be making us insensible to conventional arms. The memory of Hiroshima is greater that the memory of Vietnam. How we wish that conventional weapons were given the same respect as to nuclear arms! How we wish that killing many people little by little, day by day, were as objectionable as killing many in a single day! Is our world so irrational, that if the atomic bomb were possessed by every nation and the destiny of all depended on a single lunatic, we would have more respect for the use of conventional arms? Is it thus that universal peace would be more secure? Is it our right to forget the 78 million human beings fallen in the wars of the 20th century?

Today, the world is divided between those who live in terror of being destroyed in a nuclear war, and those who die daily in wars fought with conventional arms. This terror of the final war is so great that it engenders a frightening insensitivity to the proliferation and use of non-atomic arms. It is urgent that we fight as much to prevent another Vietnam as to prevent another Hiroshima.

Arms do not fire themselves. Those who have lost hope fire them. Those who are dominated by dogmatism fire them. We must fight for peace without dismay, and accept, without fear, the challenges of a world without hope and threatened by fanaticism.

■ In San José with the President of Mexico, Carlos Salinas de Gortari.

With Margarita
and the Mexican
poet Octavio Paz.

I SAY TO THE POET

The Peace Plan signed by the five Presidents faces every kind of challenge. The path of peace is difficult, very difficult. We in Central America need the help of all to achieve peace.

It is easier to predict the defeat of peace in Central America than its victory. It has always been easier to predict defeat than victory. So it was when man wanted to fly, and when he wanted to conquer space so if was during both wold was. So it was, and is, when man tackles the most terrible diseases and the task of eliminating poverty and hunger in the world.

History has not been made by those who predicted failure, who renounced their dreams, who abandoned their principles, who allowed laziness to stultify their intelligence. Those who at times have fought for human triumphs have always been accompanied by the spirit of their peoples, by the faith and destiny of many generations.

103

Perhaps it was in hours as difficult for Central America as those in which we live today, perhaps it was in premonition of the present crossroads, that Rubén Darío —the greatest poet of our America— wrote these lines with the conviction *that history would change its course:*
Pray, generous, pious, and proud;
pray, chaste, pure, heavenly, brave;
intercede for us, supplicate for us,

for already we are almost without sap and bud, without soul, without life, without light, without Quixote,
without feet, without wings, without Sancho and without God.
I assure the immortal poet that we shall not renounce our dreams, fear wisdom, or flee freedom. I assure him that in Central America we shall not forget Quixote; we shall not renounce

life; we shall not turn our backs on the human spirit; and we shall never lose faith in God.
I am one of five men who signed an accord, a commitment which consists, in great part, in the act of desiring peace with all one's soul.

■ With former President of Costa Rica, Daniel Oduber; President of Spain, Felipe González; and President of Venezuela, Carlos Andrés Pérez.

On returning from Oslo.

106

President Arias greeting Ted Sorensen, former adviser to John F. Kennedy at a dinner in Gracie Mansion, New York. Behind, Ed Koch, Mayor of the City of New York.

In New York with Bernie Aronson, US Undersecretary of State for Inter-American affairs.

President Jimmy Carter on a visit to President Arias at his home.

THE ARIAS FOUNDATION FOR PEACE AND HUMAN PROGRESS

FUNDACION ARIAS
PARA LA PAZ
Y EL
PROGRESO HUMANO

■ María Eugenia
Penón, Executive
Director of the Arias
Foundation, and Edson
W. Spencer, President
of the Ford
Foundation.

■ Visit of the members of the Council on
Foundations to Costa Rica.

FOR PEACE AND THE POOR

In San José, with Mother Theresa of Calcutta.

I have come to plant a seed and to renew a commitment. I have come to deliver thirty million colones from the Nobel Peace Prize of 1987. I have come to tell you that I donate this prize in order to help combat poverty and other manifestations of violence. I give it to reaffirm my unshakeable faith in the ways of peace, of freedom, and of democracy.

This seed that I plant today is of the fruit we gathered yesterday. It is the story of peace, of a free nation. It is the story of democracies in lands dominated by tyrants. It is the story of the teacher and not of the soldier. It is the story of law and not of arbitrariness. It is the story of dialogue and not dogmatism. It is the story that speaks of a nation that triumphed in a battle for peace without threats of tanks, without betraying a beautiful past, without renouncing the forging of a future full of hope.

The Arias Foundation for Peace and Human Progress which we are inaugurating today, cannot turn a neutral face to our history and our future. The peace that we enjoy today must be passed, stronger than before, to future generations. But that will depend on the courage and the imagination with which we defend our values, and on the justice that we are willing to guarantee to those who suffer from loneliness and poverty. For us, nothing could be more beautiful, nothing could have greater significance, than the struggle to defeat poverty in the name of peace.

Margarita campaigns for the protection of the Costa Rican turtle.

■ In her capacity as Chairman of the Board of the Arias Foundation for Peace and Human Progress, Margarita signs the constitutional act. To the right, Dr. Alvaro Umaña, Minister of Natural Resources.

WE HAVE HAD ENOUGH WARS

Explaining to children the reasons for his struggle for peace.

■ On the streets of San José on December 1, 1987 during the celebration of the
«Day of the Abolition of the Army» in the company of his wife Margarita
and Jim Wright, Speaker of the House.

A NEW LIBERATING ARMY

José Figueres symbolicly destroys the armory in Costa Rica, on December 1, 1948, the «Day of the Abolition of the Army».

Changes are taking place in favour of freedom. It is urgent that these changes taking place in the nations of America permit the consolidation of democracy, and the rebirth of hope in development. We need a new liberating army. We need the soldier to abandon his rifle and take up a plough. We need the soldier to commit himself to the freedom of his people and not to the violation of its rights. We need the soldier to understand that two democracies have never been at war in all of the history of Latin America.

In a work session, during a discussion of the Central American Peace Plan.

TO STRUGGLE FOR PEACE

■ The five Central American Presidents in the Guatemalan city of Esquipulas.

I am not afraid to say that peaceful methods will always be superior in the struggle for the re-opening of a newspaper that has been closed, or of a jail where an innocent man has been imprisoned. We cannot resurrect those who have died in war. We cannot ease the pain caused by the violent death of a loved one, or appease the hatreds that have been generated. All regions of the world with a similar history know that this is the most effective way to create unending conflict.

Years of hatred and millions dead in Iran and Iraq. These two nations have acquired additional centuries of poverty, and it will take equally long for their scars to heal. What did war resolve?

Years of hatred and hundreds of thousands dead in Afghanistan. They will be even poorer, and will walk the sad paths of mourning for the friend and brother and mother lost to violence. What did war resolve?

Years of hatred and thousands dead in Angola. They will be even poorer and there will be no future for their young. In years to come, they will speak of the past, of the men and women who fell, of those who came from distant lands to propagate grudges. What did war resolve?

Years of hatred and thousands of brutal deaths in Northern Ireland. They kill each other in God's name. The valleys are no longer green for the children who are born in these lands. The stamp of hatred is the inheritance of the past. What did war resolve?

Years of hatred have clouded the incomparable beauty that has pervaded the world since Machu Picchu. The heights that captured the poet's imagination are now symbols of incomprehensible violence, of nameless cruelty. The heights have been cloaked by murder and death. What has war resolved?

Years of hatred and thousands of deaths mark the trail that condemns El Salvador, a destroyed

and prostrate nation where only silence greets a mother's lament and a child's suffering. How much more pain, how many more deaths must be endured before reason and mercy will return? What has war resolved?

How many have disappeared in Argentina or Uruguay? «Where are they?», ask the mothers. But they receive no response. The sorrow of these mothers stems from seeing violence turn the dreams of their children into nightmares. What has war resolved?

Years of hatred and thousands dead in Nicaragua. Who would think that this was the land of Rubén Darío? What explanation will he who kills for the sake of oppression give history? The lament of Nicaragua will not be immortalized by the poet: it will be experienced by its young and many other generations. What has war resolved?

The Central American Peace Plan is in good shape. From the very beginning, some claimed that this peace initiative had no future. From then on, every day, there have been some who continue to claim that it has no future. Fortunately for Central America, the predominant political issues in the region revolve around the Peace Plan. We have always recognized the magnitude of the obstacles we need to overcome. We have always known challenge to be a better risk than the alternative.

Today's obstacles are different ones, although as great as those we faced when we began the long path toward peace. We are on the threshold of peace, in that area of half-light where we don't know if the next step will take us into the light or back into darkness. We know the desired path: the respite must become a cease-fire, a cease-fire peace, and peace a new social, political, and economic order that will permit the eradication of poverty, and the freedom of all nations.

There are powerful forces which are angered by the Peace Plan, powers that have wanted to use every delay to justify war. They are the same forces that first pressured us not to create the Peace Plan, and now pressure us to denounce it. Those who encourage war do not have the moral authority to judge efforts for peace. We have accomplished more in one year than they have accomplished in many years of war.

If the wounds that we are attempting to stanch in Central America had been made recently, if the memory of rancour were fresh, and the repression and poverty that have divided the Central American peoples were superficial, we could say that twelve months is enough time to wait for reconciliation and a new vision for democracy.

However, we could justly say that there has been a guerrilla movement in Guatemala for a quarter of a century, that El Salvador has not seen an end to the shedding of innocent blood for nine years, that Nicaragua has been the home of inauspicious opportunism since the 1930's.

Since the dawn of Central American indepen-

dence at the beginning of the 19th century, this land of lakes and volcanoes has not known peace. The periods in which the Central American peoples have been permitted to forge their own destinies in peace are measured by years, not decades.

I ask myself why, when we have been willing to devote so much time to war, we aren't willing to give peace a chance?

The world is changing and we not only must change, but must do so more quickly. Peace has been encouraged by almost all of the countries and leaders of the world. Only fanatical minorities on the left and on the right continue to maintain that Central America should continue living outdated ideologies. There is neither law nor justice in those few who have chosen hatred and turned their backs on the new world that is emerging in Latin America.

The world of the future is one of freedom for all, without distinctions. Let us cooperate with men who are free and who seek freedom. Let us tear down walls, wherever they are found. Poverty cannot continue justifying the dictatorships of the right or the left. Let us demand together the right of the poor, men and nations, to be free.

The sorrow of the tango that is heard in Viejo Almacén, will never stop shouting for freedom! Machu Picchu, up above, will eternally shout its rebellion against the paths of terrorism, darkness and death.

Whoever supports violence in Argentina or in

Peru, in the North or the South, is a traitor to the people of our lands who demand democracy. Men of peace can look back without becoming salt statues. We are obligated to understand history and committed to changing it. We live in a world where courage is required, not to go to war, but to fight for peace.

The person who seeks peace, with the instruments of peace, is accused of being deluded, a dreamer, naïve. What does it matter! The new world, the world we have sought for two thousand years, is the world of the naïve.

There are those who refuse to descend from the Sierra Maestra and others who refuse to retreat from the barracks. Both are obstacles to freedom and development. The lands of Darío and Neruda are captive and I want to see them freed. From Mexico to Chile, the countries of Latin America have waited for two hundred years to embrace each other in democracy and freedom. The peoples of the Americas reach out to the liberating hand extended by Bolívar.

Ten pages are left to be written in this century. We can make them pages for the freedom of man. Let us fight for them to be written without blemish. The cause of freedom belongs to

us all and does not recognize borders when its shield is reason and its sword is diplomacy.

We must fight for the advent of the day in which every Central American will lift his head and look to the future with optimism. That is a day which we cannot give up. It will be the day when every government of the region will forever respect human rights. It will be the day when fear of freedom will be lost and the majority will be free to govern. It will be the day when dialogue will triumph. It will be the day of peace, of development, and of democracy.

 In Managua, with Farid Ayales, Costa Rican Ambassador to Nicaragua, Commander Tomás Borge, Nicaraguan Foreign Minister, Miguel D'Escoto and President Daniel Ortega.

ADVANCES IN THE PEACE PLAN

■ In the Presidential Office with representatives of the
Guatemalan National Revolutionary Union (UNRG).

■ The Representatives
of the Farabundo Martí
Liberation Front (FMLN)
meet with President Arias
in the Presidential Office
in San José.

■ Meeting in the
Presidential Office, in
San José, with US Assistant
Secretary for Inter-American
Affairs, Elliot Abrams;
US Ambassador to
Costa Rica, Dean Hinton,
General Collin Powell, and
Costa Rican Foreign Minister,
Rodrigo Madrigal Nieto.

Visit with Cardinal Miguel Obando y Bravo in Managua.

Once again at the United Nations, analyzing the progress of the Peace Plan.

AT THE GATES
OF PEACE

As President of Costa Rica I came to the United Nations for the first time in 1986. I said then that Central America was on the brink of war. I have returned today, for the last time during my term of office, to tell you that we are on the verge of peace. Yesterday, I came to ask for your help. Today, I come to thank you. Then, we had to end a war. Now, we must build peace. How quickly the world has changed in these few years! Bloodshed between brothers has ceased in many places on this Earth. I ask myself: Where are the winners of these wars? Where are the losers? We should not be afraid to say it: the only winners were those who had the courage to sign a peace accord; the only winners were those who had the courage to rectify history. Wherever violence continues, everyone is the loser.

It takes very little to turn the peace of one day into the violence of the next. It is also true that individuals and peoples can make a difference in favour of peace. The strength of forgiveness and dialogue can silence the guns and put everyone to work for real solutions. Our destiny is not carved in stone. It is our responsibility to create a different future.

The Central American Peace Plan continues to move forward. The presidential summit meetings in El Salvador and Honduras have strengthened our commitment to fight for the end of violence and the improvement of democracy. The armed struggle in Nicaragua has come to an end. Thousands upon thousands of young people in that country owe their lives to that courageous agreement. An electoral process has begun and, in February 1990, the people of Nicaragua will elect a new President and Parliament. With the help of many and with international supervision, elections in our sister country will be fair, and equal guarantees will be given to everyone. We must continue to foster the reconciliation of the people of Nicaragua:

With the famous American soprano Jessey Norman.

■ With Spanish President, Felipe González.

the return of those who are in exile, the silencing
of the guns that are still being fired, the end to
violence as demanded by reason, mercy, and the
Peace Plan.

THE CHAINS
ARE BROKEN

The brutality in El Salvador has not led to any
solutions. Let anyone in this room rise in the
presence of the nations of the world and enu-
merate the problems that were solved by those
who encouraged and supported violence in my
tortured Central America. I ask all those who
are able, to help bring an end to the senseless
killing and destruction in El Salvador. We
demand the end of a decade of pain which has
yielded no gains and no future.

In the last few years, the balance in Central
America has tipped in favour of freedom,
democracy and peace. Much remains to be
done. We are very far from achieving the political coexistence that we seek for every country in
the region, but we are moving in the right direc-
tion.

The best proof of this is the United Nations,
which in the last few years has again begun to

shine as a centre for international diplomacy. Its voice has the authority of the majority and breaks the chains which once bound it to the extremes of power. Politics cannot consist of manipulating our fears or of the art of exaggerating our differences. We can respect it only when its purpose is to achieve agreement.

As I said to you at the beginning of my speech, I came to thank you because the success we have attained would have been impossible without your help. You are giving a human face to a world that until recently knew no mercy. I leave with the joy of knowing that peace is closer at hand and with the confidence of knowing that the slum which still darkens the horizon in my country will disappear. I will always be a Costa Rican at the service of these causes and your ally in these struggles the world over.

A NEW WORLD

A new world emerges before us. The will of the majority is starting to prevail. Dialogue has regained its strength as a way to find solutions to the most difficult of the conflicts that confront us. Peace accords have been signed that have silenced the guns in Central America, in the war between Iran and Irak, in Angola, and in other places of the world. Soldiers who no longer have a purpose in faraway lands are beginning to return from empires and their satellites, making one more contribution to the peace of Africa, Europe and Asia.

In San José, with Costa Rican born astronaut Franklin Chang Díaz.

■ Vice President Dan Quayle visits President Arias at his home. Arias' wife Margarita, his brother-in-law, Agustín Penón, and his son Oscar Felipe accompany him.

A CENTURY OF DEMOCRACY

■ The opening ceremony of the «Plaza de la Democracia» in San José,
with the Prime Minister of Canada, Brian Mulroney and the Presidents of Uruguay,
Julio María Sanguinetti, and of Argentina, Carlos Saúl Menem.

ONE HUNDRED YEARS OF FREEDOM

Oscar Arias inaugurates Inter-American Presidents Summit.

Today, men and women everywhere are re-embracing democracy. Few are those also can proclaim the freedom of their people, to forge the new destiny, to outline its basic features, and to breathe into it a new spirit. The ruler with revenge in his heart has no place in this new order, any more than does the ruler bent on settling the scores of the past. The ruler whose hands are stained with blood or tainted by drugs or corruption has no right to govern any people. There is no place in the new democratic order for dictatorship and evil.

When I began my term of office, I called for an alliance for freedom and democracy in the Americas as a necessary prerequisite for a new era of peace without hunger. It is a pleasure for me to welcome here today men who have led the return to democracy in their countries. But the task is not complete. There are still authoritarian governments and tyrants still hold sway. To the shame of freedom, we still have dictatorships of fifteen to thirty years duration in our continent. As we encourage the electoral processes which open new opportunities for democracies, we must use every diplomatic means possible to ensure that not a single tyrant remains in power in the Americas.

Because Costa Rica has made a pledge to work for the new world of the future, our political commitment is to change. We salute the courage of those who have begun the process of nuclear disarmament and conventional arms reduction. We are determined to replace Central America's history of war and violence with peace and freedom. I am grateful for the help you have given us in this undertaking. I appeal once again to all of you to use diplomatic pressure for the silencing of guns and the pursuit of dialogue. Because we support change, we favour a strengthening of the Inter-American political system. May everyone sit at a table so that we can work together, within a regional diplomatic framework, to address our common agenda.

Thirty years ago, the visionary Venezuelan statesman, Rómulo Betancourt, proposed that

■ In San José, with his friend John Biehl.

free nations break political and commercial ties with authoritarian regimes in order to promote freedom and democracy. Forty years ago, the visionary Costa Rican statesman, José Figueres, dissolved the Costa Rican army in order to promote development and democracy. Perhaps we can now say to Betancourt and Figueres that the moment has arrived when together we will isolate dictators, that the time has come for disarmament and we will work together to that end. One hundred and eighty years ago Simón Bolívar dreamt of a single, united America. Today we see Europe embarked on an unprecedented path towards economic and political union. As the Berlin Wall comes down, there will be no distinction in Europe between rich and poor, prisoners and free men. We see the birth of a huge market which will bring together the peoples of Canada and the United States. Perhaps others will join, overcoming language barriers. We should not lose this opportunity for peace, nor should we simply imitate what others have done. We want to form, and should form, a part of the solution to today's problems. Perhaps we will also say to Bolívar that there will be an America in which all persons are free.

During the Inter-American Summit with José Azcona Hoyo of Honduras; Rodrigo Borja of Ecuador; A.N.R. Robinson of Trinidad and Tobago; Hugh Desmond Hoyte of Guyana; Julio María Sanguinetti of Uruguay; Brian Mulroney of Canada; George Price of Belize; Carlos Andrés Pérez of Venezuela; José Sarney of Brazil; Alfredo Crisitiani of El Salvador; Daniel Ortega of Nicaragua; Carlos Saúl Menem of Argentina; and George Bush of the United States.

THE SUMMIT OF THE AMERICAS

In San José, with his wife Margarita and the President of Venezuela, Carlos Andrés Pérez.

This final decade of the 20th century offers an unparalleled opportunity for understanding and development. Two thousand years ago, one man sought peace on Earth among men of good will. So far we have given him not a single century free of war. We should not pass up this opportunity. The common agenda which we have before us is of concern to us all: democracy, development, disarmament, debt, deforestation and drugs. We have it in our power to end an era of fruitless confrontation between nations. We must commit ourselves to the opening of new windows for opportunity, to working together in the search for common solutions to common problems. We must chart new courses in tune with the hopes and aspirations of young people everywhere.

We, the leaders of over 700 million people, have come together. We have not come to unveil a plaque or to inaugurate a monument. We have not come to sign declarations that will be forgotten even before they are passed on to posterity.

We can no longer be the prisoners of a minority, regardless of the strength it may find in drug corruption, the force of arms, the brutality of violence, or the cowardice of terrorism. We are going to build the homeland of the democrats, the great homeland of Bolívar, the homeland of the peoples with unlimited freedom, the homeland of the majorities who will never punish dissenters. America will walk without fearing freedom.

We will work together to build democracy, to foster development, to alleviate foreign debt, to combat drugs, to preserve the environment, and to accelerate the process of disarmament. We want results and we will be faithful to this agenda because it is the mandate of our people.

■ Brian Mulroney, Prime Mini of Canada, George Bus President of the United States, greet the Costa Rican peopl with Preside Oscar Arias.

In the National Museum with Presidents Bush, Menem, and Sanguinetti.

A PLAZA IN REMEMBRANCE

This is the same place where, forty years ago, José Figueres Ferrer abolished the Costa Rican army. This was once a military barracks. Today, it is a museum. Here, reason defeated force. Here, the fearless tolerance enjoyed by a people without arms was born. Here, the soldier became a teacher; the rifle that once hung over his shoulder became the book now held in his hands. To receive our American brothers in this place, is to receive them in the very heart of Costa Rica. It is to

Julio María Sanguinetti, President of Uruguay gives a present to President Arias.

With José Sarney, President of Brazil.

receive them with the open arms of a hundred years of democracy.

We have come to proclaim a new spirit; to inaugurate a plaza which, on its first day of existence, celebrates its one-hundredth birthday; to free a new attitude; to fearlessly proclaim our desire to understand one another and work together. Let us not deny that the world has changed.

In this plaza, children will sing songs and poets will recite poems. Painters will display their works and students will play. The elderly will rest and lovers will embrace. Never will the echo

of a soldier's boots sound here. Neither will tanks pass, nor regiments march. Combat planes will never fly overhead.

This plaza belongs to the history of American democracy. Today, the people of Costa Rica proudly offer to the Presidents who visit us, the freedom for which they have struggled and the peace for which they have longed.

It has been said, my good friends, when there is much to achieve, words must be short. Long and splendid have been these 100 years of liberty. Generous is the presence of the Presidents

and Prime Ministers who accompany us. Long and splendid has been the affection of Costa Rica. We listen to the joy of liberty. We listen to a free people in the streets and countryside, to the liberty of one hundred years of democracy. We say to the youth of America, that we do not only claim that all humans will be free, but also that from this point forward, we swear to fulfil this sacred promise in San Jose. In this plaza, constructed in tribute to the liberty and the democracy of America, will remain the souls of one hundred years of free men and women.

The leaders take a break during the Inter-American Summit.

Work session.

■ Press conference
with President Bush.
Also present are Costa
Rican Foreign Minister,
Rodrigo Madrigal and
US Secretary of State,
James Baker.

146

The President of Uruguay, Julio María Sanguinetti, dedicates to the Costa Rican democracy: «I say today that where there is a Costa Rican, no matter where he is, there is freedom».

With
Carlos Saúl
Menem,
President of
Argentina.

■ Accompanied by various Costa Rican students.

■ In San José with a group of actors during the International Theater Festival.

THE PRESIDENT
OF PEACE *

It isn't surprising that the Nordic countries revere the same ideals that Oscar Arias has made his own. It is a hopeful paradox that, despite the geographic distance and the language barrier which exists between us, we speak the same language and feel very close to one another.

There is yet another reason that we, the Nordic countries, give a wholehearted welcome to the President of Peace. He is a living testimony that even small nations can count with great leaders and play an important role in global society; that, despite being small, we have a responsibility, as much to ourselves as to others. President Arias' goal will also be ours: the peace and welfare of the people.

The time when a country could isolate itself from the violence, injustice and war existing in other parts of the world is gone. Our globe has become too small for that. We should hope, then, that a new era will arrive when those leaders who defend peace will also be sculpted in bronze and placed on a pedestal like the war heroes of times past.

President Arias is an impatient man, not for himself, but for all of those who are the victims of war. He has only four years as President because the President of Costa Rica cannot be re-elected. This fact gives him more authority and integrity. No one can accuse a Costa Rican head of state of thinking of his own re-election. This fact also contributes to increasing an already impressive credibility.

In spite of his haste and impatience in the service of a good cause, Oscar Arias has made a pledge to persuade and not vanquish. This is the fundamental difference between the somewhat slow method of democracy and the misanthropic efficiency of dictatorship.

* A toast given by Jo Benkow, Chairman of the Storting, given in honor of Oscar Arias on the occasion of the 1987 Nobel Peace Prize.

Original title in Spanish:
Horizontes de paz:
El aporte de Costa Rica a la pacificación
de América Central

Translators:	Bernice G. Romero and Joaquín Tacsan.
Supervisors:	Ralph Voguel, Monica Washington and Francisco J. Aguilar.
Presentation, selection of texts and general coordination:	Jorge Emilio Regidor Mattey.
Spanish texts supervisor:	Mariángel Solera Víquez.
Editorial direction and design supervision:	Renato Cajas Corsi.
Graphics and concept model:	Pierre Eppelin.
Color separation:	Sepacolor de Costa Rica, S.A.
Printers:	Litografía e Imprenta LIL, S.A.
Photographers:	Gilbert Córdoba, Sigurd Pérez, William Esquivel, Roberto Morales, Matías Recart, Javier Guerrero, Rick Friedman (of Black Star), Jason Bleibtrev, Ivonne Barreto, and the Associated Press, United Press International, France Press, Sygma and J.B. Pictures; archives of the Costa Rican newspapers: «La Nación» and «La República», and «The New York Times Magazine» of the United States of America.

A publication of
the Arias Foundation for Peace and Human Progress
San José, Costa Rica, 1994.